Glaciation

Also by Will Stone

Poetry

Drawing in Ash – Shearsman Books (2011; Shearsman edition 2015)
The Sleepwalkers – Shearsman Books (2016)

Translations

Les Chimères – Gérard de Nerval – Menard Press (1999)
To The Silenced – Selected Poems of Georg Trakl – Arc Publications (2005)
Journeys – Stefan Zweig – Hesperus Press (2010)
Rilke in Paris – Rainer Maria Rilke & Maurice Betz – Hesperus Press (2013)
Nietzsche – Stefan Zweig – Hesperus Press (2013)
On the End of the World – Joseph Roth – Hesperus Press (2014)
Poems – Emile Verhaeren – Arc Publications (2014)
Poems – Georges Rodenbach – Arc Publications (2015)
Montaigne – Stefan Zweig – Pushkin Press (2015)

Will Stone

Glaciation

Shearsman Books

This second edition published in the United Kingdom in 2015 by
Shearsman Books
50 Westons Hill Drive
Emersons Green
BRISTOL
BS16 7DF

Shearsman Books Ltd Registered Office
30–31 St. James Place, Mangotsfield, Bristol BS16 9JB
(this address not for correspondence)

www.shearsman.com

ISBN 978-1-84861-458-1

Glaciation was first published in the United Kingdom by
Salt Publishing, Cambridge, in 2007.

Acknowledgements

I would like to thank the editors of the following esteemed publications in which some of these poems first appeared:
The London Magazine, Agenda, Poetry Salzburg,
The Wolf and *The SHOp.*

This book is dedicated to the poet
Michael Hamburger
(1924-2007)
in fond memory.

Contents

'The glaciers creep like snakes that watch their prey, from their slow rolling on; there, many a precipice, frost and the sun in scorn of mortal power have piled: dome, pyramid, and pinnacle, a city of death, distinct with many a tower and wall impregnable of beaming ice. Yet not a city but a flood of ruin is there that from the boundaries of the sky rolls its perpetual stream...'

– Percy Bysshe Shelley

'Mont Blanc – Lines written in The Vale of Chamouni' (1817)

The Oaks

In May the oaks on the ridge thicken
strangely towards evening.
They begin to command, take over,
they rope in the hedgerows, they deepen.
When the flaring of the human subsides
the owl's amber eyes stare out
from the cage of contorted branches,
to follow the field mouse carrying corn,
while we slumber, the hunt goes on,
and in the morning
the dewy blooms deceive us.

You sit beneath their dusty branches
and calmly seeds parachute into your hair.
For once you might see with those eyes,
connect, rake over, receive answers.
But they are unable to signal.
Our worn out bellowings for meaning.
drift uselessly up into their canopy
and are snuffed out, saved from themselves
like the staggering flames of spent candles,
from the dream of some deliverance
that limps stoically in our wake.

Restoration

On palm-fringed paradise islands
over creamy sand and through
polluted surf the real ocean abandoned
this extinct generation still plays on,
unaware that plans are in the final stages
for its obliteration. Brazen,
they dump their sacks of organs
by perfectly azure pools and poised
leap up from white springboards.
Beneath palms, confident in their wealth
they lounge, as they have always done,
lost in the lack, lured to the shallows,
all the effluent that darkens the earth
from the outflow of their shadow.
But above them unseen the moon's ice scythe
is sharpened, to the stars are handed weapons.
All the planets and terrifying expanses
of nothingness gradually synchronize.

When the powerboats stutter and their
engines stop,
when the flight is grounded and can
no longer take off,
when the barbecue coals refuse to glow,
when the maid fails to sweep the patio,
when receptions are abandoned,
and the guests' mail remains unopened,
when shoes left out are set adrift un-shined
on the dark canals of hotel corridors,
when the breeze lifts parasols and waves
begin to curl like great silver razors,

when the horizon's guillotine sweeps down
held in the vice of sea and sky
and untended children like heralds cry,
you'll know its not the end of time
only restoration.

Winter Light

All grey, the diamond glass
and distant estuary, mercury
that once crept into the cold snare
of land and stayed there.

No relief in the graveyard for souls.
An icy wind keeps the spirits
pressed to the clay, and hoar frost
ravishes the inscriptions.

But from the marsh the cathedral emerges,
and the first flame of gentle hymns rises,
an amateur choir, a feeble congregation
beneath the angels' powdered faces.

The beautiful gift of their decay.
Nailed there, saturated with prayer,
they bless the terrified birds outside
losing strength in the black hedges.

The Heart

At school they held it up in a jar
I saw the purple ventricles and aorta.
I saw the human heart passed along
in buckets stretching weedy arms
to end in a hiss of steam and sweat,
the sly contempt of flames.
I saw the valves, one with a kink
and felt the shape of that lumpen thing,
and heard the nervous statements of students
as the stainless steel sunk in.
I saw the heart fail or thunder on,
a flayed horse bursting through a copse
and hearts that wait in bone-armoured chests
I've seen them wave hopefully
like the silken tendrils of sea creatures swirling,
forever reaching into a dark green void.
And I saw people target the heart
and once in a cemetery I even saw one rise
somehow gasping to the surface.
But no one heard the cries or cared
when mercifully I smothered it.

Van Gogh's Room

Gutted cell
the skylight dominates.
Two long walls, two short.
An opening for the door.
There we linger I and the guide
where he came in each night,
eyes red from strain and corn dust,
sat on the narrow bed,
stacked still warm canvases
beneath, then sleep.
He bled grey one unnoticed afternoon,
bled from the wound
in under tree shadow that darkened
the delirious journey back.
The deep poppy red was blood.
The yellow a movement
the whispering failed to follow.
But now besotted fans file in,
they scale the winding stair
and shuffle there,
walk in walk out,
turn around, go back down,
convinced their hero suffered well
in seven different languages.

Pigs

At dawn they come,
their watery eyes peering through slits.
The trucks lurch, their wheels
sink into the soft ploughed earth.
Then the pigs trot down muddy ramps,
snouts puffing steam,
mouths half-open as if laughing,
for suddenly they are free
to stand in the puddle meares
of their prison and slump down
in crude hooped huts of iron.
Soon the bare field is crowded
with bacon.
The ghetto proceeds unknowing
to its destruction.
In flattened straw fresh piglets
squeal and frolic.
Carefully the farmer counts them
and the sow looks up at him.
He slaps her flank in thanks,
then walks away.
Months later I returned.
The field is bare, freshly ploughed,
nothing remains.

Swifts

Powered by screams
and the black bat twist of their wings,
they slice through the insect cloud.
Heavenly dogfight, no quarter given,
the plunder ravished unseen.
Round they come again,
cyclists on a bend
clinging to their manic carousel.
The air cannot hold them.
The sun slips from their sleek
gunmetal backs.
They are gods.

Storm off Speke's Mill Mouth

For Paul Stubbs

They herd the cliff, the dark shoal,
spewing from their gunwales
the foiled assault, the broken surf.
Aroma of terror, hardening silhouettes
rising from the sea as if for shelter.
Wrecks, bellowing bestiary
shoved into grey coves
to be plundered of sanctuary.
Spume boils, undoes itself
under the heel of malignant cliffs
at whose top the mad hair of bramble dances
in the broom-sweep of a fresh squall.
Black axe-heads embedded.
These storm mockers plant their knees
more firmly in the moraine.
Helpless you stand above them,
held by the wind's strong hands.
Nothing before or beyond.
Only a lost shoe flattened on an outcrop,
the hair of drowned sailors, still knotted,
riding the foam.

Morwenstowe

Follow the seaward pull of the coombe,
check your high speed against
the buzzard's calm.
He steers above the sunken lanes, a king.
Stationary now, his shadow hook
drags through the lambs.
The monks once learned
from his anchorite toil,
they left the wildflower seeds,
the path, the stone step-stile.
Their voices still decant the wind
that worries the tower,
where Reverend Hawker stood in awe
and went to build his driftwood hut
above the rock-chunk clustered shore.
And peaceful there, far from men
wrote some poems.
He seized the storm and filled with joy
watched the elements
make room for him.

Trakl – The Oval Photo

Autumn, the return of empty tumbrels.
On the heavy anvil he laid his heavier head.
Between dense matter and the hammer
Blazed a grid of unseized stars.

When molten metal came raining down
Doomed ducks rose from a lonely pond,
For the final first time fully cocked
Boys slowly circled all the blood.

Approach of a storm.
Outline of a body in white chalk.
Warm winds whip up straw, gentle dunes
Hold spent lovers hard against the shore.

Like a swollen sack the body falls,
As resting gulls drift towards
Rusting jetties where late men saw
The extermination of all rational thought.

The Commander

On the Steppe in high summer
he was the commander.
His lean brown face rose from the turret
issuing orders.
Fattened on the fall of France and eager
his faithful men below obeyed,
their single panther sucked into
the field grey slick that swallowed Ukraine.
Now, a year on, he lies in a frost-lined pit,
mummified like a pharaoh in strips of blanket.
Calmly he watches a family of field mice
devour his blackened toes,
while outside they plant the hacked off horse's leg
as a signpost in the snow.
'Hölle' it reads, with a crude arrow pointing
whichever way the wind is set to blow.

Russian Fair Play

After they crossed the Oder
a band of Russian troops
captured an SS Scharführer.
In a bombed-out house stood an
untouched piano.
They sat him there and gave him
the following orders…
'Play you scum, but if you stop
we'll finish you off!'
The man then played for sixteen hours
until he fell exhausted
across the keys.
The Russians showed no mercy
and swiftly carried out their promise.
They dragged him from the ruins
and as his cramped hands clawed
at their filthy greatcoats
shot him.

Glaciation

After Shelley's 'Mont Blanc'

Once handed over by the deities to death,
we truly began to live, glacial.
Now, cut off in our ice holes
we listen to the creeping snout,
the slow cracking of human hearts,
lashed rafts almost submerged by pain,
that somehow are carried down
between steep walls of rock,
before whose primeval malevolence
the earlier explorer turned insane.
Birds cry out sadly as they wheel again
back and forth over the sucking abyss,
over the monstrous plaster limb of ice.
Here where firs are snapped like twigs
and huge boulders weigh their anchors
to set out on endlessly repeated summer nights,
or in winter when fresh shale and rock
peppers the dull blue ice, and wolves
drag tattered scraps of carrion about.
Against the waxing moon they unleash
their white snarls, then sated run into the forest,
the dark dust spaces, to sleep side by side
licking each others bloody faces.

And the huge cables quiver mournfully
on their towers, where in clusters
the little cars huddle together.
But they are lifeless, deserted
and all around tall firs sag with snow.
There is no way through.
Only the relentless flow of unseen rivers

in deep icy fissures, where the leathery bodies
of the ancients are strangely preserved.
Crows form a thicket on a lonely mountain road.
At the cars approach they rise with reluctance.
In the slipstream the fur of the carrion faintly stirs.
A hungry prey is hunted by hungrier wolves.
We do not see the kill, nor the ice move
and in summer's thaw leave its passengers
polished skulls in clear rock pools.
Vainly the climber hacks into the ice wall
and the explorer sinks his nation's flag.
Nothing remains of their inexplicable straining.
Only the ice moves, a snake slowed by feeding.
The ice moves and shackled, relentless,
slave winds groom her awful surface.

Verhaeren in Rouen

They left the conference in high spirits.
He said farewell and popped into a Confiserie
for some lemon sweets.
Those who had met him watched him
descend the iron clad station steps.
They could not go down
to the seething platforms where,
as the last train for Belgium crawled in,
the crowd surged towards the machine.
Then the slight poet was swept along
and in a panic tried to mount coach 7607,
but as the train was still moving, mistimed
and merely clutching air dropped down,
between the next carriage and the platform,
down to the wheels which unceremoniously
lopped his legs off above the calves.
They got him out but all in vain.
There he lay losing blood, fading fast.
As a crowd thronged, those closest heard
him in a murmur say these words…
'je meurs, ma femme, ma patrie!'
Then, leaving his vast estuary of poetry
glinting gamely far below, he sighed
and calmly bled into the ocean.
Alerted, the station master came running…
but by then the victim was gone.
In his breast pocket someone found unharmed
that last-minute gift for Marthe,
the lemon bon-bons.

The Ceremony

Night has fallen.
You leave the bright foyer
of the tourist hotel
and enter the shadow canyons
between cathedral and churches,
where pious song and murmuring voices
leak from closed convent rooms
and the past with surprising tenderness
slips its furtive hand in yours.
Inside the cathedral ranks of candles blaze,
a miniature army of glinting spears.
In the stalls a few stragglers
bow their heads to pray,
then abruptly step out as if saved,
kneel on icy flags to cross their breasts,
or else light candles and peer
into the dark caverns of soaring arches.
They look for some sign,
but their pain simply slides off the Virgin's
face like thawing snow.
That is enough for them.
Service over, the priest clears up.
With practised certainty
doors and gates clang shut,
psalm numbers shuffled away.
Like the last dregs
you are drawn with the rest
through the porch door into darkness.
Abandoned once more
the ashen Christ sags helpless,
hooked like a haunch of meat
facing the incision decision and
swift sword-sharpening of butchers.

Exhibit ‘B’

For Leon Greenman – Auschwitz survivor 98288

The last tin of Zyklon B
sits in a window no one sees,
has been emptied,
holds only the air inside,
the stale air of the museum,
the air taken from them.
This round tin in which
one might place a cake freshly baked
or leave on a garage shelf,
a dusty crypt for nails.
But this round grey tin is here for good.
It exists behind the glass for us,
is proof, is meant to say;
observe my grinding vacancy,
peer right in and guess the crime.

Imagine all this contained,
the most effective powder
a German firm was proud to offer
clients who needed six or seven
to erase a thousand naked humans.
The treatment commenced.
In twenty minutes
together they died alone.
The last tin of Zyklon B
is a grey tin with German words
clearly inscribed around the outside:
GIFTGAS-ZYKLON B
Prayers were rushed and then they died.
They died and prayers were rushed.

They tipped this tin, the 'orderlies',
came in the van that showed the red cross
and when the people were firmly sealed in,
they climbed onto the roof
and tipped that tin, they tipped it right in.
The survivors rally awhile and fade,
for this tin a poet jumped in the Seine.
They took his mother.
Another fell from the stairs.
That was later, after he had become
a successful author.

This tin holds too much.
this tin overflows with air,
last concerns of mothers, an old man's sigh,
polite requests of cripples burnt alive.
So regular that rounded shape,
each curve equal to the next;
a functional circumference of death.
So carefully the tin was tipped.
Nothing wasted.
A hand moves, motion completed.
Task begun and accomplished.
Diligence, decency, obedience.
A song bird's call from a nearby wood,
rain darkens the roofing felt.
You can now make out
the absolute silence of God.

Stroke Unit

Late afternoon.
They come for their loved ones
down fiercely lit corridors
so mopped and buffed
they'll never record those who passed.

Plodding on past lifts and wards,
the birth of trolleys through double doors,
little gardens trapped in sunny shafts,
even a chapel, hoping, door ajar.

Then they arrive at the stroke unit,
barely noticed by busy nurses
sowing their jocular brusqueness,
tying behind them abruptly
their apron strings of plastic.

Six beds and in each a man
born between the wars.
Remember their names:
Dick, Reggie, Les, Stan, William, Walter.
Barely a word spoken,
but how well they know each other.

Wearily they watch their neighbour
raised and lowered. Passing clouds,
privacy curtains drawn then opened.
Nil by mouth and a name
in black marker pen
on a plastic wipe-off board.

Far away, on the other side
of the wall, the women.
In each bay an inert form, no sound.
Only the dark stewardship of machines
and at one end the exuberant sun
blundering through a blind.

The Wrecker's Coast

Winter dusk over the Atlantic.
Sermon of a lunatic
scrawled over anvil cloud escarpments.
A lone crow touching down,
then hoisted up then down.
Only the blind feel the laboured
black lettering.

The wind is grinning,
a grey fox chasing out warmth,
while pale ghost fish fathoms down
settle on a victim, mouths open
so certain, the gleaming ornament
of their ancient eye
trapped in the timer's darkness.

Smooth approach of hearses.
Men you saw only yesterday alive
hammer on the glass from inside,
women who walk past laid out,
their one chance to rise
when iced hands thaw on breasts,
abdomen, thigh.

Only to freeze over yet still clawing out
through fabulous crystal
and free to meet the frosted copse
where blue smoke gently rises
and hearing delicious crackling
you check all's clear, run in
to pocket the first bolting flame.

Cinders slow, ebb to the odd
lick of a lighthouse beam
limping out there to Lundy.
Sinister wave slope and the dark screes
at the forbidden quarry we once explored.
The derelict equipment on which
childish hands trespassed,
caressing cobwebbed wheels
once heaved by whistling men
who are dust.

The Sniper's Victim

I believe she was the third victim
and was sitting quietly on a bench reading.
She was reading her book in the sun
when the sniper struck.
She was singled out at random
on a Monday morning in a small town.
No-one knows why.
One moment she was alive
and about to turn the page,
then her head exploded.
The book fell to the concrete,
an abandoned hand twitched.
She was left draped in a blanket
waiting for forensics.
She had chosen to wear sandals
because it was such a warm day.
Beneath the clumsy shroud
I saw her pretty tanned feet.

Angelic Intervention

For Stephen Romer

Like the sail silhouette
which stymies the vacant horizon,
or the person
who half enters my room
to stand late-flowering, vulnerable
by the open door,
she wells up from the grey
weather of people.
We choose the same moment.
Our feet touch.
Only once the frail rendezvous.
Just in time she comes to.
Gone.
As the current pulls
the crowd stamps out all evidence
of our affair.
How long could I remain there?
An uncertain image on her eyelids,
given up in a shop window
so cursorily.
I turned round then
and they shielded me.
The overworked angels raised
their matted wings.

Translators of Baudelaire

At their desks the translators pray
on early winter afternoons.
Sonatas seep in from the other room.
A door opens and in slips the cat,
whose eyes an infuriating green,
are later seen at a misting pane
by an immobile owl outside.
Behind the hunched-over translators
the moon makes its first rough sketch
on the back of the sky.
From dark bushes birds sweep
the last flurries of song.

Inside, the translators of Baudelaire
bail out their precarious craft.
Their navigation is rudimentary.
No fabled tributary leads to gold -
the way is less clear, everything a deception.
The jungle of living language is shrieking,
beasts are prowling the steep slopes of rhyme.
Every possibility wrestles with decay.
Above, the heavens flaunt their stars,
overwhelming and pure, ice that holes
the skiff carrying the anguished brain
before the mighty march past of the
alexandrines.

Your mind
a log that turns in sluggish currents.
Language
a line of heroes, you the translator

are violating in too hasty an honouring.
You hold out your hand, but theirs is a glove
filled with air, the heart answer is elsewhere.
A hospital ward airing in spring.
Lines of metal beds on which lie cripples,
the translators of Baudelaire.
Doctors lean over the faintly twitching forms.
Famished veins quiver at the slightest chance
of a new approach. Perhaps now…
Into the original they dive again
and like flowers bent by rain they rise,
assured they will be the ones to bear
the irresistible bloom.

Exploring Culture's Wreck

For Paul Newland

Danger! – treacherous sunken wreck…
One must be qualified to go down there,

amongst the glittering shoals that come and go
at mass produced café tables, as in Soho, where

the inebriated tramp with filthy paws and matted hair
lurches near and all draw in their cappuccinos,

those loud little cogs who 'love London life',
imagining themselves at the centre of some

movement going in the other direction
from putrefaction, these hardy carrion

who stride with such confidence from
Costa to Pret, jabbing at their little phones,

gorging on galleries, ticking off shows,
those who hunt for gossip like crazed wolves

and crave fame at any price, the horde,
ever present, myopic feeders fanned by the

digestion of all they devour, the males,
the females and their anatomical weaponry

that snuffs out vision with alacrity, I fear
their eternal presence has the finality

of the crushing fall of a dead horse.
And death is there as always, riding high,

counselling the newcomers, who fumble
with their flag of hope the wind ultimately ignores.

And most are concerned with vanity,
ego-media-mania and the spawn of celebrities.

But like spiders charging at the slippery porcelain,
they'll not escape life's rushing flood,

which eventually catches on their spindly legs
and carries them off like doomed sailors

into the whirlpool, the hungry plughole,
the omnipotent and understandable abyss.

The Ghosts of Tully Castle

All were slain save for the Humes
when the Maguires took the bawn
and thrust their flag
into still-warm musket holes.
Sixty fell to the Irish sword,
man, woman and child cut down.
Perhaps their hot blood redrew
the cobbles here,
where now we admire the formal
herb garden.
Beneath the belly of the tower supports,
an exuberant bay
continually pesters the stone.
Abandoned facades soar darkly
to their tapering cowls.
In their apertures lie bundles
of sticks,
a timber yard for crows.
The ghosts of the murdered are long
swept out.
But cloven skulls that tumbled
from the thicket of raised blades
are somewhere here,
perhaps where the hyssop flies its blue
pennants, or the golden marjoram,
or under this unfamiliar questioned
between my fingers.
Revelation; lemon balm.

Schopenhauer's Reprieve

They had assured him of silence,
but he was disturbed.
Roaring, he burst through like a train
and following a tussle
threw the still chattering woman
headfirst down the stairs.
At first I judged such a harsh penalty
grossly disproportionate to the offence.
But having read with much enthusiasm
'The will to live' and 'on the vanity of existence'
I think his action perfectly legitimate.

Heym's Madness

Now he struggles,
his hands fastening on the current.
A paleness dotted with dark islands
bobs horribly beneath the frosted ice.
An eye peers through, drawn out.
He trowels his verse and builds a house
that begins its life as a ruin.
He goes in winter to the undertaker.
He ducks under the snagging boughs
of their laughter,
racing home breathless to revolt.
Heym.
You have never heard of him,
but his heart spit builds each year
along the city's metal shore,
though he falls evermore
onto the sharp spike jeers
of the rabble.

Grave Detail

Late August in Westward Ho!
and the blue Hydrangeas are dead.
Only spectres are left,
glimpsed between nicotine nets
in the Braddick Holiday Home.
The breathing follow this season's coffin
through the smell of frying,
past the gaudy entrails of the Co-op,
scooped back in at closing time.
Past the beach shop where they hung
carpet slippers and flip-flops,
spasmodic offerings to a putrefied God.
Past the giant plastic ice cream cone,
quivering in the salty wind, future
toys of the devils' charred children,
firm favourites for the idle curiosity
of annihilation.
Beyond, the cauterising ocean where
waves lift the surfer's seal heads,
pointing them back to the orange and red
tracer of amusements,
slow moving shadows behind plate glass,
diners, craning their necks above
the rising pestilence.

Reading of the Bourgeois Women

Hair streaked with ash,
or blonde blown-dry to a weary fragrance.
They look to the reader,
livestock staring from a field
patient before the dull insistence
of unresolved cancers,
futile affairs, straying husbands.
They watch the lectern-steadying
of their associates.
A confession has been formed from emotion.
Without wings it dies there on the lectern.
A punch of feather falling down plate-glass.
In being read, a shot deer whose skinny legs
quiver then collapse.
But the kill goes unseen.
The ranks as one break into applause
a chocolate box of 'ooh's and 'aah's.
They relate to the suffering endured by the other,
they desire to go no further.
In the interval, bathing in chatter
and warm chardonnay,
the herd's cyclopean eye
rises periscope-like above the din
to fix on its cornered prey,
the publisher.

Regeneration

First we were shown pictures.
Ruins of suburban homes,
rooms open to the sky
with what looked like people inside
living on as if nothing had happened.
Some gathered round a fireplace
or television,
their waxen faces pretending
the fantasy fire's fingers
touched them.
Others sat at a table spooning dust
and ash into their mouths.
In the rafter-strewn hallway
a priest and doctor in earnest dialogue.
Next door a child in pyjamas
praying by his bed, an embryo of faith
exposed to a billion stars.
In the background always that nimbus shape
watched by cripple windows,
bullying the remaining space,
dark pendulum,
a politician's fist above the podium.

The Ipatiev House

4 a.m.
Time to bring them down.
But unseen, by the back staircase.
Tsar and Tsarina, heir and princesses
slipping out from sleep's pale traces.
Gradually in the girls fists a cross germinated,
and the heir clutched his mournful father's
severed hand.
Doctor and maid prised away from purpose,
lingering over responsibility,
helpless insects wandering between the panes,
they filed into the brutally lit cellar room,
drawn into the drain, their measured step
overcome by the choking vine
of the darkest century's rank entrails.

In a vague line they stood
as if for a photograph. Alexandra,
raking over the ashes of her petulance
breathed out dust; 'What no chairs?'
They were duly brought and stood
ridiculous, stiff-backed, crimson, flawed.
She slumped down, lost a moment
in the dawn stretch of distant cannon.
Soldiers half-dressed, sweating vodka
poured in, eyes wide with awe
'It's them, him and her, the whole lot!'

The captain's voice, wire thin, arrogant
ceremoniously launched his official statement.
A judge made bolder by the jury's long delays,

his final rhetorical flourish to level the pistol.
'What?' the father heard but did not hear,
then his brains flecked the pale lips
of his daughter Anastasia.

Onset, cordite, Lenin wanted it…
hands to faces before a thorn of bayonets,
Bosch's time-hewn faces spewing malices.
Baying they skewered them to the floor,
but kicking, twisting forms endured.
The jewels sewn into their corsets parried
the lunging grunts, the roars.

In their lace petticoats the children rolled
through their own gore, flapping hens
fished for by the fox's snapping jaw.
At last they lay still, a bare knee twitched.
Despite 'strange resilience' the heir's crushed skull,
kerbside fruit unwanted, undone by a cartwheel.
In sheets prepared they bundled them,
but too suddenly fresh, confused, the blood
bloomed through, signalling
futile aftershock speech unread.

Carts carried them to the remote forest.
No possible language raised them
from the floor of the dank shaft
they tipped them down, no rescue flame
no trumpet sound, all too near
the fires of the whites left only cold ash,
the evil celebration of a frozen dawn.
Silver birches, the way they fell and rested
and for eternity felt the murderers meat hands
sliding over their still shocked faces.
At the Ipatiev house in the half light

they held up the royal dresses.
They smelled the soap, caressed the underwear,
tore the little prayer books to pieces.

The Hawk

Between grinding carriageways
sixty feet up, hovers the hawk.
Totally focused, she has located
slim sustenance and readies herself
as oblivious mankind goes by
into the roaring asphalt void.
Unwavering the hawk hangs,
over the blackened rubber shreds,
the grit of coloured glass,
the coarse weeds and sickly grass.
Suddenly a speck of blood and bone,
she wobbles once
before dropping down,
torn by a choice of gusts,
talon outstretched, eye immense,
brimming with kill.
Even here the struggle, unseen horror,
enjoys its prop-filled arena.
The old routine played out
near a length of broken exhaust
and a blown tyre.

The Buzzard

Descending in loose coils
he hollows the coombe,
hones the lamb-studded meadow,
the weir where the brown Exe foams.
He's the landowner,
the headstrong kite
tugged by the child's wonder.
He's the governor,
quivering powerfully as
the train shrieks under.
He's in no rush
to provide a sublime silhouette,
drag into art some mundane stump or post.
Later, perhaps his dark cape will drop
to unsettle the gargoyles,
or enable the silence
stored in the heart of a lonely tower.

Natural Phenomenon

He clears a section of the Marylebone Road of rubbish,
piling high his trolleys with our dead skins.
Then he sits where he drops, cross-legged
like a fractious tot,
or a grounded bird a dawn away from death.
Horns blow, gibes, abuse is hurled.
But this one has left our world and his dark
Moorish eyes are used to dragging a spear.
Up and down he goes, a grubby hand
reaching down to gather in the harvest
of all that falls beneath the saw whine sound,
off-cuts of our apocalypse.

Garden and Leisure

Between us a perspex dome,
then above me a greater one.
Russian dolls – unlucky beings
detained indefinitely,
the lop-eared rabbit and I.
"Ah – how cute!" shrills a girl.
Derangement has afflicted the bunny
who cannot move, only vaguely senses
heavy rain clouds loom, pointing fingers,
the eager peering in,
sad cycle of light and shadow.
Immobile by his little house
on a bed of wilted lettuce
and his own dirt
there he twitched, the exhibit,
the sweet one, unit of consumption,
condemned to life
with no parole.

The Sinister Blue Lake

Served by stillness, it laps its blue lip
over a shore of darkening clay,
that strange lake in the foothills of the alps
near the goat village of Les Lindarets.
No-one dares swim there or paddle,
the children hang back and only one
brave boy risks a black pebble.
But when that suicidal speck is sucked
soundlessly into the blue abyss,
they seem unsettled and move on
elsewhere with their picnic.
Those mysterious unseen depths
solid blue and opaque, concealing
the slow motion of unknown creatures,
sickening fish and hallucinations.
The urge to stare at that heavy turquoise plate
with its curdled milky edge, and fall
drained by the silence within its circumference.

Greyfriars

Late afternoon is the time for that path,
when the light fails and the iron gates of Greyfriars
eerily brand the shadow with cowled monks.
It's best when the light fails down that path
skirting the meagre cliff top copse,
where in February a brook of snowdrops
bubbles up, and the balm of sea sound
rolls back beneath the bridge with its baby arch.
Inexpressible melancholy drew them,
Thomas, Fitzgerald, Swinburne,
their footfalls weighed, compressed, absorbed
by thick fir foliage and the slow scrape of birdsong.
Rhododendrons, dark peat paths and sounds
flickering on dead leaves, frail skeletal feet
or the first drop feelers of a downpour?
You proceed due east to the light.
Suddenly the land has had enough,
shrubs long extinct fling themselves out,
strung with cries and madly racing cloud.
You face once more that icy scythe of slate
lipped by jaundiced surf, the gore of cliffs,
the sluiced shore where horses plod,
heaving the dark barrows of their blood
northwards then south.

The Jetty

At the first sign of your presence –
a groan
and as your purpose wakes the
idle supports,
bellows.
Such histrionics!
The vast lake gathers the sounds,
smothers the familiar intruder.
All is calm.
Your white legs sink into the water.
It's easier to live from the moment
your skin signs a pact with the cold.
Perhaps the rest of you
could slip below,
to be fitted in the chain-mail shoal,
those slow falling coins,
oblivious alchemists
of the untrodden crypt.
Or withdraw and retreat,
leaving the platform weightless
but for invited breezes,
their gentle down
moulting off the lake.

Hour of the Old Buildings

Surprised by the sudden greening of parks,
pitted hulks form up,
edging towards the lack of us,
feeling at dusk towards the new life they'll lead.
Their lonely windows high up have long since
lost the habit of a face,
but still reflect their proud architect's retreating step.
High up, abandoned to dust
and shadows of unwary moths,
they spawn the emptiness
of all their busy tenants cannot know;
the diminishing feet, the ownerless dog,
abandoned crumbs,
last week's newspapers swept along
then grabbed by railings
to cover the shame of an empty playground.
Keen to unload the future event,
they welcome the homeless to their
stygian basements, where, beside warm vents
they whisper through night
to the bagged-up foetal forms.
Come morning, they disgorge around the city
their wild sermons.
But no-one looks up at the old buildings
or sees the haunting maze,
the dead canyon-makers they'll become.
Their high windows indifferent to all
that passes below,
black ticker tape, and a trickle
of madmen.

Sudden Flight

Then the boy noticed the flag of white plastic
signal in the shallow stream. He remembered
that was where the shy brown trout had once been.
Strips of charnel maize, set aside, mournful,
falling back even as the pale pennants struggle
in decay seasoned with shades of sunflowers
flickering on the east wind, and over there
dumped fridges flaunting their rusting pipes,
a mildewed sofa upended.
Three fields away on a rise the slow copses,
great barges barely moving
in the winter field waters,
topped with hoar frost or snow
for a novelty cargo.
Birds spring abruptly from fresh cut hedges
some flailing machinery had mauled.
They lead him along the lane,
before handing on to others, guides
who only falter at the border they know,
then disappear on wild air streams
darting fast like cinders.

Where the Waves End

Relentless
is the sad competition of the surf,
rolling in so proud
then astonished to be broken down.
Unable to warn followers
who rise to mimic,
rush in and receive the black rock's blessing,
the same ill treatment.
I have lain here an hour
and many have expired,
cocky generals on white ponies
trotting sideways down the slope.
Found by cannon, in disarray,
they fall without a word,
or, rudely awoken, charge off, headless.
Bulging nets of black rock
squeeze the incomers out.
They reset their traps quickly
before the next one bearing down
can see its fate.
Curiosity coaxes them
into this strange production,
churning out vacancy
under a fine mist.

The Monk's Bell

Almost smothered
in the bindweed of sound,
with prisoner precision
the monk's bell still chimes.
In vain the sunflowers shout,
flame burst dragging its murder skirt.

Like executed Amazon trees
even they go down in screaming
petrol storms of sawdust.
But the monk's bell still chimes
through the scouring rush hour traffic,
the pilot's sly application of air brakes
long before the northern approach.

Once this village was remote, rural
and strangers were held at the turnpike
by berry-stained locals.
Now it's stubbed out
by our death bright world,
a lingering act of remembrance,
a wandering leper with a bell.

Inconceivable is the survival
of that sound.
On the hour pale chimes wave
from their captive tower.
Doomed survivors in a dark hull
bang a block of wood against the iron.

The planes stack up.
Flies find their place on the corpse.
But still those soft ripples head for shore
to melt on us old lags lying here,
skewered by the heat of our desert.

They are a songbird's appearance
on the prisoner's ledge,
dew sucked from the grass
by those thirsting to death.

SS Fort Breendonk

In memory of W G Sebald

As today when the reeds rustled on the moat
no-one listened.
Men like us but not like us howled
only for the ears of the others, the rest
who howled inside and drew blood unseen,
whose fingers bored into the mildewed brick.
One screamed 'I'm too young to die.'
But the guard replied 'This is hell and I am the devil!'
He was a seventeen year old burglar from Essen.
They propped the condemned at the stake,
and afterwards got the Jews in
to collect the clogs, hose down the posts.
And birds sang after the execution,
as was the custom.

Now I go down these surgical tunnels,
so straight the time taken to proceed
from one end to the other at walking pace
cannot be measured. Drawn into
this echoing mine where nothing remains
but the squandered sound of tape recorded
voices, screens with grey haired men
droning on in ill-lit cells to no-one.
Death comes, the statistics…death
His meaty hand chose the torture weapon.
All language was fluff, the names… the names…
In order to knowingly exist he had to beat
with his truncheon that body until lifeless,
calmly enter it like poison, unchallenged.
Then to the SS mess for a night of song
and a snapshot to celebrate the execution.

'The complexities of human nature are displayed here.'
states the tourist literature.
'We welcome schoolchildren.' And
'It must never happen again.'
That sort of thing, or else the ardent witness
who recalls the commandant's dog named 'Lump'
left seventeen bite marks on the body.
This is where a man fell, and here, one of us
though we cannot be sure of their names.
The butcher leads a prisoner past spooked
whitewashed walls, springing back pain,
this way my lad, now it's coming...
The unfurling joy of freedom miles away.

In a gloomy recess the inadvertent sculpture
of discarded coffins embossed with a cross,
left for those who three days in fell across barrow
or later swung remorseless from a rope,
giving a last superfluous Hitler salute,
or filed from a court room in the roar of the void,
or heard whatever remains in the prison yard, only air
and the looped barking of dogs, virtual spades
clattering in the shadows of buttresses and blind spots.
They found a belt buckle near the sentry box,
The words they could only just make out
through mud and rust –
'God is with us'.

Frithelstock

At sunrise the rooks return to Frithelstock tower,
tie their soot ribbon around the outside,
into lichened apertures send their cries.
They graze the ivy shadow,
dark islands of evergreen they do not see
but where their mournful cries take root
and as atmosphere unite
to keep intruders from the *via dolorosa*,
the lime tree path
leading down to the lost priory arch.
Three lancets there, whose crumbled contours
present themselves for air, not glass.
Three morose guards whose orders lapsed
now let the sleet, the storm,
the breeze pass through
and the bats.

In Boulge Churchyard

I am safe beneath
the warm brick tower of Boulge,
amongst those gentle tombs,
their grassy tunics
loosely buttoned with early cowslips,
or passing through the gate
of rusting wrought iron, that leads
into a field of fresh young corn.
Fitzgerald's rose still flourishes
beside the mausoleum of his familial foes
and the snowdrops each year as ever
play their communal trick,
and each year they get away with it.
Cheerfully they flourish by path and grave,
though later they'll prepare for death,
they at least felt the breeze on their necks
and truly knew the sun.
Then they are gone and I too must leave,
following the ruts in darkness,
nudged onto the brute modern highway
as behind me another acorn falls
to scuttle down the quiet avenue of trees.

Explanation to an Academic

She who lectured on Beckett
expected more from a poet.
It's getting late, she said
perhaps a steely prose is required.
I explained.
Poems are trapped passengers
unable to decide how to tackle
the assailant.
You see them through
the grimy windows of the page.
You see the still-born poems
necking embalming fluid,
anything to forget how intractable
the knife,
how many fresh worms swim
gleefully in the wound.
I pointed to a vast empty hangar.
There in a corner they pile
the limbless dreams.
Those without them –
mammon's white chieftains,
drive the stake deep in.
But even they rip a leaf from a hedge
and inhale the aroma of it's broken life.
Even they worry about their lame dog,
work an arm steaming with blood
around their sleeping wife.
Even they, in decay's grey wash
surface their shark snouts
to tear at the vacancy
for a mere soul sinew
a rib of love.

Sorley

A slug of lead stopped Sorley,
his head thudded on a sandbag softly.
Once more death had driven them
out from the sunken lane,
and the sun deserted the blasted stumps,
passed them all by, the Suffolk dead,
their muddied photographs, their pay unspent.
The poet's kitbag revealed its poem
as wearily he fell in line with those
he had shadowed who would not signal,
but only picked more up like fluff,
or snow to an unfinished snowball.
He wrote something on that last day living,
but the dying pestered him unknowing,
as when storm flies worry the jaded rose
brooding on deletion, all in strict procession
moving helpless in the scented evening
to the close of their brief lives.

At Hartland Point

Here the thump roar deepens,
pistons rising, falling,
driving out a darker space.
Unsettling sounds, spent seasons,
chased from primeval chasms.
Here where nature conducts
a derangement of elements I stand,
explored by the vast wind
that tunnels in for morose meetings
with rock wall where black ore spews
and white powder bursts from fissures,
streaming purposeless to ashen shale
three hundred feet below.

Down to dumped rocks,
piled around the shore's pale neck like shot,
cruel slabs sluiced as you turn away,
by tidal waters racing in
for long-dead channels craving sound
and above, sickly turf on a gentle rise
peeled back by the storm's finger.
The asphalt of service roads,
of pathways split and gored, blistering up,
a branch unable to hold,
man's efforts to anchor, futile.

Cast like all else on the dark conveyor
of winter nights
down to the beach, the crude lip,
a dice throw of broken bricks
from some long-collapsed emplacement.

Combines of surf thresh at the headland's base,
brawn of land that flings
the seabirds round like flakes.
Huddled in their cars the visitors wait,
rocked by the gale, silent, having seen the drop
and the terrifying deception of screes,
or an ocean's obsession glimpsed
through the wreck's timber-fanged wound.

Stragglers

The sunflowers still face east in death.
No-one has told them
their bleached fronds are hanging broken.
Perhaps a bird's weight will help draw them
gradually to the ground.
No-one shall come and admire them,
or spontaneously decide to steal them,
rushing back to the car with their looted flame.
Only a few drab pheasant hens and partridges
bark feebly around their husks.
The whole field has discovered perfection
in giving up.
All will fall by December, scythed by frost.
Massed grey limbs will litter the patch,
empty seed heads upturned who stare
at that milky socket where a beleaguered sun
fumes uselessly in the traps.
Even as they go down and before the final
humiliation of the plough,
a few last seeds might creep away,
heroic stragglers who somehow brave
the ebony machinery of rooks.

Ducks and Geese

First the geese
tottering their pottery bodies,
sumptuous patterned vases.
Heads of coal with a smile of snow,
happy nooses moving back and forth.
They sway through the old mallards
parked on the down-speckled grass,
green heads pitted, past their best,
turrets turning sadly on the breeze.
Then tucked in behind
as if forcing a secret
into the pressed crowd of feather
and drowsy plumage.

Reeds in November

In November they reach
homeward rooks without touching them
and the water spreads to the muddy edge,
paint on silk, blood in a shoe.
The reeds choir escaping air,
the seen nutrient their brittle gills
loose over walkers, sculptures, watchers.
They lean in a wave then rise
supporting the body that bypasses us
and dies out as arranged
in the space between
competing gulls.

The Deserter

They tied him gently and slipped
a flour sack over his head,
the deserter whose friends were dead.
Have you anything to say before sentence
is carried out? declared the Sergeant
I… I… would very much like to hear
my wife's voice.
From the misty field of sprouts
a crow's black caw broke out.
They pinned a scrap of paper
over his jerking heart.
The crude coffin sat ready on a cart.
A collapse of shots,
heaving through the dewy air.
Twisting once he slumped to shoulder
his unfinished cross,
until they cut him down.

In St Sulpice

Through the grey light of the nave
the new coffin comes,
a pale slug on the asphalt path
that of a sudden brings revulsion.

The drone of a priest rises
echoing in the dark chapels
and the dead wings of language
settle in a web-bound corner.

A man makes the sign of the cross
and leaves with his wife.
Eagerly their hearts pump on
and they link arms for a few more years.

The congregation lower their wreaths
like the banners of a defeated army.
They stand with heads bowed
as a muted siren limps in from the street.

A few tourists slip in and give way
to pious souvenirs, or step into the gloom
of the side chapel where Jacob wrestles
with an angel against the mildewed stone.

Arrival and departure go unnoticed.
Exit and the shrill fountains claim you.
Pigeons land like a cloak thrown down,
spray of grain from the sower's hand.

Take Off

Our turn to face the ramp of air.
One hoof kick and the airport
is a worn out child's toy, a useless replica.
The golf course reveals its shame –
landscape gouged, unseamed, for
a glint of blade swung by the unseen.
Then the ocean, nicked by ships,
the slow agony of their bow wave,
against our tyrannical speed.
Who are we, now we have ignored
the blunt warning of the woods,
the relentless counselling of streams,
the sonorous caution of stone?
We who for warmth try to light
the sand of our desert.
We who live now in the full glare
without the blessing of a shadow.
Only the dead have a record,
an entry made by a suicidal angel
buried deep in their files of ash.

Exodus

Over dunes of abandoned hearts
the fleeing clamber.
Hearts left behind like heavy packs,
cherished dolls, silver candelabra.
Some abruptly add to the mound,
placing their pump like a stone on a cairn.
The wind snatches their wishes,
severing the windpipe at once or
dumping them in a pine forest crypt.
A few priests refuse the ascent.
They kneel at the bleeding edge,
mechanically placing wafers
in the defenceless mouths of the dead.
Everywhere hastily vacated vehicles,
ox-carts, tumbrels, stretch limousines.
In these forgotten babies on their backs,
beetles kicking their little legs.
In another a gaggle of jaded porn stars
smoking crack, and unrecognised
a media baron devouring his own face.

On the other side the sea,
calm, immense – the controller.
Desultory attempts to launch coracles
entertain the breakers.
But most sprawl on the shingle,
tracing words in the sand of the foreshore.
Hawkers pass by,
peddling a few last lustful cries,
a moment of vision, or if one can afford it
some unforeseen sweetness.

Some chew seaweed mournfully
or watch white crabs
take up residence in their heart space.
All day more arrive, blackening the shore,
staking their claim with wild gestures
the rest ignore.
Only at dawn does the tumult subside,
the realisation roar of confinement,
when they scan with red-rimmed eyes
the horizon's wall for a door,
a faint mark of oncoming prows,
the bliss of burgeoning loud hailers.

But there's no foothold in that shimmering rock
and smothering their still struggling dreams
they sink down one by one
onto the point of the sun's keen lance.

Webern's Last Cigar

Exhaustion his destination,
somewhere in the mountains
away from all not foreseen.
Hunched, briefcase bulging,
bones of a score showing through,
swept along with the rest –
the degenerate refuse,
to remote hamlets where
sallow goatherds stared
and an obscure evil that arrived first
settled in the soft rain of bells.
On the 15th of September
he dined with his daughter
and stepped out for a smoke.
He saw the empty pasture,
the dark pine vault and the moon –
a dead tramp's leaking eye.
The American soldier loomed.
'That's contraband. Stop, I'll shoot!'
He lit the match.
It was a fitting occasion for
a Gregorian requiem mass.
Only five followed his coffin down
past the droning apple boughs –
across the wasps' shop floor,
to the paupers' mausoleum,
fresh earth incision scenting
the stationary bergs of mountain air.

October

Mother and father have aged.
Those Picardy walnuts lie in the bowl
slowly turning to dust.

Over the next rise they see the summit,
their exit, they see nothing, like humankind
where forever the new veins run

rushing their revolution cargo
to the habitual answer of black marble.
Each movement inspected by the hunger
which smoothly takes over at birth.

Signs of winter and each time the bare tree
stands there alone, the moon
is a madman's palm pressed against glass.

Dawn at the edge deliberates, then resigned
overwhelms the darkened town.
Sleeping children breathe deep.

They cannot know the ash of loss
already dusting their rosy feet.
They simply step over

the organs, those anchors
that drag them down later,
and the urge to sprout, reproduce…

Or become melancholy alone in a house
sustained on calm resignation,
following the dark shoals of books
which outlast them.

www.ingramcontent.com/pod-product-compliance
Ingram Content Group UK Ltd.
Pitfield, Milton Keynes, MK11 3LW, UK
UKHW041632190726
13854UKWH00006B/2459